ILAN RAMON

ILAN RAMON

ISRAEL'S SPACE HERO

BARBARA SOFER

✦ LERNER PUBLICATIONS COMPANY / MINNEAPOLIS

To Yaakov, our children, children-in-law, and the next generation
—B.S.

The author wishes to thank those who shared their beloved memories of Ilan, as well as their expertise and knowledge of flight and of Israel: first and foremost to Eliezer Wolferman and Rona Ramon, and to Liora Etzion, Esther Gussarsky, pilots Danny Grossman and Michael Lior, Tamar Zemech, Dr. Reuven Segev, the staff of Yad Vashem, and General Amos Yadlin. Thanks also to editor Judye Groner for her devotion to this project.

This book is available in two editions:
Library binding by Lerner Publications Company, a division of Lerner Publishing Group
Soft cover by Kar-Ben Publishing, Inc., a division of Lerner Publishing Group
241 First Avenue North
Minneapolis, MN 55401 U.S.A.

Website address: www.lernerbooks.com

Library of Congress Cataloging-in-Publication Data

Sofer, Barbara.
        Ilan Ramon, Israel's first astronaut / by Barbara Sofer.
            p.   cm.
        Includes index.
        Summary: A biography of Ilan Ramon, Israel's first astronaut, who died when the space shuttle Columbia exploded during re-entry in 2003.
        ISBN: 0–8225–2055–9 (lib. bdg. : alk. paper)
        ISBN: 1–58013–116–6 (pbk. : alk. paper)
            1. Ramon, Ilan, 1954–2003—Juvenile literature. 2. Astronauts—Israel—Biography—Juvenile literature. 3. Air pilots, Military—Israel—Biography—Juvenile literature. 4. Columbia (Spacecraft)—Accidents—Juvenile literature. [1. Ramon, Ilan, 1954–2003. 2. Astronauts. 3. Columbia (Spacecraft)—Accidents.] I. Title.
        TL789.85.R35S65 2004
        629.45'009—dc22   2003015257

Manufactured in the United States of America
1 2 3 4 5 6 – JR – 09 08 07 06 05 04

TABLE OF CONTENTS

An aerial view of the town of Beersheva in 1961

★ Chapter 1 ★
CAMELS FOR SALE

Ilan Wolferman was new in Beersheva, a town on the edge of the Israeli desert where the sun shone most days of the year. A man with a red and white head scarf was leading a camel right toward him. "Want to buy it?" the man offered.

Riding high up on the camel's back sounded like fun. Some kids were afraid of heights, but not Ilan.

But what would he do with a camel? There was just enough room in their apartment for Ilan, his mom and dad, his older brother Gadi, and the piano!

The Wolfermans had moved from Ramat Gan, a suburb of Tel Aviv, when Ilan's father Eliezer went to work in the Dimona nuclear plant. Ilan was in second grade.

Ilan means "tree," but there were few shade trees in this hot town. David Ben-Gurion, Israel's first prime minister, promised that one day Beersheva would be a major city and play an important role in Israel's future. But when Ilan was growing up, it was mostly a quiet town. Every Thursday, the Bedouin Arabs who lived in tents outside the town came in to set up a street market with shining jewelry, coins, sheep, donkeys, and camels.

A crowded section of the weekly Bedouin market in Beersheva

Israelis and tourists from abroad came to shop. Ilan and his friends got used to seeing the Bedouin men with camels and the women wearing veils.

Ilan attended the Be'eri Elementary School. There were nearly 40 boys and girls in his class. The language at school and on the playground was Hebrew, even though many of his classmates spoke different languages at home. Their parents had immigrated from Morocco, Iraq, India, Poland, Hungary, and Romania.

Ilan's parents spoke Hebrew at home. His dad had come to Israel from Germany as a teenager and had fought in Israel's War of Independence in 1948. Ilan's mom, Tonia Kreppel Wolferman, had been imprisoned in the terrible Polish concentration camp at Auschwitz when she was 19. She didn't talk much about that sad part of her life. She wanted her children to be happy and smiling and not to think about her suffering. Mrs. Wolferman loved music and gave piano lessons.

Like most Israeli children, Ilan studied music at school. His teacher would write the words of the songs on the blackboard and play the accordion. The children would copy the words into brown notebooks, decorate the pages, and memorize the songs. Memorizing came easily for Ilan, but he enjoyed solving problems even more. His favorite subjects were arithmetic and nature,

**Israeli schoolchildren in the 1960's
help tend a vegetable garden.**

which included learning about science, and hiking around
Beersheva. He studied desert vegetation, especially the
plants that managed to grow even though they had little
rain. Once a week, the class went to a field where they
tended a garden of tomatoes and cucumbers. At recess
and after school, Ilan played soccer and dodgeball.

★ Chapter 2 ★

WARTIME BAR MITZVAH

For Jewish boys, turning 13 and becoming Bar Mitzvah is an exciting time. It means being old enough to be considered an adult in religious ceremonies. Family and friends celebrate with a party and presents. Ilan would turn 13 in June 1967.

As his Bar Mitzvah day approached, other events shadowed the lives of all Israelis. In May 1967, Egyptian President Gamal Abdel Nasser expelled the United Nation's peacekeeping forces from the area between Israel and Egypt and stationed Egyptian soldiers along Egypt's southern border with Israel. Then Egypt blocked Israel's port of Eilat, threatening war. Jordan to the east and Syria to the north pledged their support to Egypt. The only direction without enemies was the west—the Mediterranean Sea. Israel's enemies vowed they would push the Jews into the sea.

In Beersheva, everyone prepared for war. Few buildings had shelters. Boys and girls Ilan's age helped dig

Students fill sandbags for the school shelter in preparation for an air attack, May 1967.

ditches and pile sandbags around them. In case they were attacked by air, everyone would go into the ditches for protection. Windows were blacked out with dark paper.

Then, on June 5, Israel surprised her enemies. Leaving only 12 planes to defend the country's air space, the entire Israeli Air Force—183 planes—participated in a mission that destroyed the fighter planes of Egypt, Syria, and Jordan. In six days, the war was over and the threat was gone. Israelis celebrated their victory.

Ilan became a Bar Mitzvah in the happy days after the Six Day War. Everyone rejoiced and shared stories of the war. In particular, they talked about the skill and daring of the brave pilots.

When they reached ninth grade, Ilan and most of his elementary school friends went on to the much larger Regional Comprehensive High School #3, also called the Himmelfarb High School, in Beersheva. The school had 10 ninth-grade classes. Students had to wear school uniforms of light blue cotton shirts and blue pants. For special occasions, such as Memorial Day, they wore white shirts.

In high school, Ilan chose to concentrate in chemistry and physics, and he was one of the best students in the class. He always did his homework, and he was very good at figuring out complicated problems in algebra and trigonometry. Even though he wasn't tall, Ilan was a star basketball player. He was a good swimmer and a fast runner too.

Every year, the school had overnight class trips, where students would travel in open trucks singing, cooking their own food, and camping out. One of their favorite places to hike was the mysterious and beautiful Ramon

Ilan *(back row, third from right)* **and his class take a trip to the beach.**

Ilan loved to hike. One of his favorite places was the Ramon Crater, from which he would later take his Hebrew name.

Crater of colored rock, 50 miles south of Beersheva. Years later, Ilan would remember this beautiful spot when he chose a Hebrew name.

Ilan and his group of friends got together on Friday nights, after dinner with their families, to dance and have fun. On Saturday nights, they went to the Beersheva movie theater and a local ice cream parlor. By 11th grade, some of them had bought used motorbikes that gave them the freedom to get around town.

Nearly everyone in Ilan's class would be going into the army after graduation. It was the dream of many of the boys to become pilots. A lot of the Air Force training

Ilan *(lower left)* **and friends pose together in the high school hallway a few days before graduation.**

took place around Beersheva, and Ilan and his friends knew every unit by the colors of the uniforms and the symbols on the soldiers' shoulders.

Ilan wanted to be a pilot, even though he would have to commit himself to spending seven years serving his country. Getting into the pilot-training course was very hard. Ilan was invited to try out.

He did well enough on his examinations to qualify. The weeklong trial course included hard physical tasks, such as running for miles with a heavy backpack, then being awakened in the middle of the night and running some more. At the end of the week, an officer stood up and read the names of all those who would continue as pilots. Ilan Wolferman was ecstatic when his name was called.

That was just the beginning. A cadet could "wash out" anytime during the 20-month training course for a variety of reasons. The Hebrew phrase is "fly away." Nearly every week, someone in the course "flew away."

Part of the course is studying physics, which was easy for Ilan. But would he be able to fly a plane?

Many pilots say that flying is a skill you are born with, and that you can't know if you're good until you try. Ilan took his first flight in a small piper cub. He was eager and nervous, but he found that flying came easily to him. He had an inner sense of how to control an airplane and good coordination. Each day he remembered to correct the mistakes he'd made the day before. He learned that for every task you need to memorize a fixed order in which to do things, and never to skip a step. Once in the air, you have to focus, focus, focus on what you are doing. You have to be strong and flexible, because when the plane turns a corner, going very fast, you feel force on your body.

★ Chapter 3 ★
EMERGENCY LANDING

One day, while still a student pilot, Ilan and his teacher were practicing loops in a two-seater airplane. The control stick that served as a steering wheel got stuck. For 10 minutes, they tried everything to move it, even kicking it. Nothing worked, and they knew they'd have to bail out. Because this model of plane had no emergency ejection hatch, they'd have to push themselves out of their seats and jump.

Ilan opened the roof. His helmet flew off. When he jumped, his leg hit the tail of the plane. He was injured and bleeding. The world was suddenly silent. He felt weightless as he arched his back and felt for the parachute knob in his pocket. Ilan pulled, and the parachute released above him making a hollow thump. He was very cold as he waited for touchdown. Ilan and his instructor were safely on the ground when the plane crashed.

Ilan had survived the plane crash, but he was grounded. He had to leave the pilots' course while he healed from his injuries. That was a very hard time for him. Would the Air Force let him continue as a pilot? His high school friend Liora met him one day in the swimming pool. "Don't worry," she told him. "If you can't make it as a pilot, no one can!"

Two months later, the good news came. He could return to flight school.

Years earlier, Israel's founding prime minister had proposed that Israelis should have Hebrew names. Like many other young Israelis who had changed their names, Ilan decided that he, too, wanted a Hebrew name. From the name "Wolferman" he took the letters "r", "m", and "n" to form Ramon, like the crater near Beersheva where he loved to hike.

In 1974, Ilan Ramon graduated from flight school and was named outstanding pilot in the course.

He loved the challenge of flying. "When you are in the air, you need to prove yourself every day. If you don't down the enemy, he'll down you. You have to

Ibexes on a cliff above the Ramon Crater

make your best effort," Ilan said.

"There is no coming in second," says the Air Force motto.

Some of the graduates were assigned to fly transport planes. Others would fly helicopters. The best, including Ilan Ramon, were chosen for the dangerous job of fighter pilot.

★ Chapter 4 ★
WAITING FOR THE F-16'S

In the late 1970s, Israel discovered that Iraq was building a nuclear plant at Osirak capable of making an atomic bomb. The Iraqi government had pledged over and over again to destroy Israel. Once again, Ilan's country was in danger.

Israel wanted to strike first. But Iraq was far, almost seven hundred miles away. The pilots would need better planes.

In 1980, the United States agreed to sell Israel F-16 fighter planes. Ilan was one of only 12 Israeli pilots allowed to fly them. He was sent to Hill Air Force Base in Utah to practice with the new jets.

The first F-16's arrive in Israel in February 1980.

The F-16's would enable Israel to destroy Iraq's nuclear plant. But there was a problem. The Israelis didn't have the special equipment needed to refuel the F-16's in the air. They would have to fly to Iraq and back on only one tank of fuel.

Ilan, then a captain in the Air Force, was given the assignment of calculating the navigation. "The target is slightly out of range," he told the mission commander with an embarrassed smile.

Ilan had to figure out how to get more mileage out of the fuel. To make the plane lighter, the team would drop their empty fuel tanks. On the way home, they would fly higher than they'd first planned. The thinner atmosphere would require less fuel.

Eight pilots were chosen for the secret mission, called Operation Opera. The youngest—Ilan Ramon—was only 26. The most dangerous position was "flying the tail," because by the time the last plane reached the plant, the Iraqis would likely have discovered the jets flying overhead and begun shooting antiaircraft missiles. Flying the tail was risky. Ilan would fly the tail.

This was a secret mission, and he couldn't tell his family or friends where he was going. At 3:55 P.M. on June 7, 1981, the first of the F-16's roared off the air base in Israel. Each plane carried two 2,000-pound bombs. The planes flew very close together so that Iraqi radar might think they were one big passenger airplane. But if they were discovered, they were low enough to be targets for Iraqi missiles.

The pilots were flying far from home, over enemy territory. The mission was very important and very dangerous.

Ilan knew the maps by heart and thought about his target. "Focus, focus, focus," he remembered.

The pilots flew 420 knots—about 500 miles an hour—just under the speed of sound—to avoid breaking the sound barrier, which would give them away. At

5:35 P.M., Ilan saw the dome of the nuclear reactor gleaming in the sunshine. The first pilot dropped his bombs. All together, the pilots had one minute and twenty seconds to complete the attack.

By the time it was Ilan's turn to drop bombs, the Iraqis had spotted the F-16's. Two enemy missiles were heading towards him. Even one could bring down his plane.

He had five seconds. He wouldn't get a second chance.

Ilan released his bombs on the reactor. Then he needed to evade the missiles. "Yank and bank" was the call. Ilan's hands moved to the control stick, he yanked it back and banked higher, pulling his head into his neck when his airplane made the sharp turn, rising to 10,000 feet. Both missiles missed him.

To save fuel, the pilots flew back at 40,000 feet. They could easily be seen and thought the Iraqi pilots would engage them in combat. But they never did. The Israeli pilots had hit the target. Osirak was destroyed. Years later, when the Americans fought the Iraqis in the first Gulf War in 1991 and in Operation Iraqi Freedom in 2003, they would be glad the nuclear threat had been eliminated.

"In the field, there are so many different things that can go wrong, that you have no way of knowing what," Ilan said later of the mission. "Things happened faster

Ilan *(top left)* and fellow pilots celebrate their victory in destroying Iraq's Osirak Nuclear Reactor on June 7, 1981. (Some faces have been obscured by military censors.)

than I expected. You don't think about anything but carrying out the mission."

In 1983, Ilan took a break from full-time flying. He decided to study electronics and computer engineering at Tel Aviv University.

One night at a party, he met a very lovely young woman named Rona Bar Simantov. Her family had emigrated from Turkey to Israel before she was born. She had studied physical education and alternative medicine. On October 16, 1986, Ilan and Rona married.

In 1987, Ilan received a bachelor's degree from Tel Aviv University. He then continued to work for the Air Force, buying and improving flight equipment such as airplanes, missiles, radar, and computers. He also conducted experiments related to flying. Over the next several years, the first three of the four Ramon children were born. All boys, they were named Asaf, Tal, and Yiftah.

★ Chapter 5 ★
A JOKE

In 1995, U.S. president Bill Clinton promised Israeli prime minister Shimon Peres that an Israeli could join America's space program. Two years later, Ilan was working at his desk when the phone rang. A friend in the Air Force was calling to ask Ilan if he'd like to be an astronaut. Ilan thought he was joking.

Until then, in Israel, if you called someone an "astronaut," it would be the same as calling him a "space cadet," someone who was often daydreaming and not paying attention.

"Come on, I don't have time for jokes now," Ilan told his caller.

Ilan's wife Rona and sons Yiftah and Tal smile with pride
as Ilan is made a colonel in 1994 and receives his epaulets
from Chief of Staff Ehud Barak.

Then Ilan realized that his friend was serious. "I have
to consult with my wife," he said. He drove home
slowly, mulling over the word "astronaut," and thinking
about what it would be like to go into space.

"When I was a kid growing up, nobody in Israel ever
dreamed of being an astronaut, because it wasn't on the
agenda," Ilan said later. "There were no Israeli astronauts.
So I never thought I could become one. When I was

selected, I really jumped almost to space. I was very excited."

The top officers of the Air Force thought Ilan would make an excellent astronaut. Being on a spaceship would be hard physically and mentally. Ilan was a superb pilot who was used to difficult conditions. On a spaceship, he'd have to live in small quarters with six other people. Ilan was friendly and liked to be part of a group. There would be many experiments to conduct in the air. Ilan was an engineer who liked experiments. And Ilan was never afraid of hard work.

At first, his name couldn't be revealed. On April 29, 1997, the announcement was made that "an Israeli pilot" would join a National Aeronautics and Space Administration (NASA) crew and go into space. He was identified as Colonel A.

★ Chapter 6 ★
HOUSTON

In 1998 Rona, Ilan, Asaf, Tal, Yiftah, and newborn daughter Noaa packed for Houston and an adventure that they thought would last two years. They rented a house, and the boys went to public school, where they began to learn English.

Colonel Ilan Ramon reported to work at the Johnson Space Center. "It's a privilege to represent the State of Israel," he said. "It's a great honor for me."

The mission was called STS-107. Ilan was part of a crew of seven astronauts who would fly on the Columbia space shuttle. The others, all Americans, were Rick Douglas Husband (the mission commander),

Ilan, wearing a training version of the shuttle launch and entry suit, floats in an emergency life raft at the Buoyancy Lab near the Johnson Space Center.

William C. McCool, Kalpana Chawla, Michael P. Anderson, David M. Brown, and Laurel B. Clark. Ilan was an experienced fighter pilot who had flown more than 4,000 hours. Still, he had never flown in space. Like three other members of the crew, he would be a "rookie," a first-time astronaut.

Ilan and his crewmates worked hard in Houston to prepare for the mission. They had to train to be in good

Ilan *(far right)*, Rick Husband, Laurel Clark, and two guides go backpacking in Wyoming with the rest of the Columbia crew to train and build teamwork, October 2001.

physical condition. They staged mock drills to overcome problems that might come up as their spacecraft orbited the earth. They practiced being weightless and learned how to eat, sleep, and work in space. The seven astronauts went to the Wyoming mountains, each carrying 55-pound backpacks with tents, sleeping bags, food, and gear to train and get to know each other. "Everything is a first," Ilan said. "Even learning to eat M&M's in space is a new challenge."

Chapter 7

WHAT TO TAKE?

Each astronaut was allowed to bring several personal items on board. Ilan wanted to carry with him something that showed the unity of the people of Israel and the Jewish people around the world. What should he take?

Ilan approached Yad Vashem, Israel's Holocaust Museum. The museum offered him a copy of a piece of artwork from its collection, and Ilan chose a drawing called *Moon Landscape*. The picture was drawn by a young teenager, Petr Ginz, while he was imprisoned in the Theresienstadt concentration camp. It showed what Petr imagined the earth would look like from the moon.

Moon Landscape by Petr Ginz

Like Ilan, Petr loved science. Inside the covers of books he had read, Petr wrote his personal motto, "science above all." In Theresienstadt, Petr had painted hundreds of pictures and edited a secret magazine of poems, drawings, and interviews written by other boys in his cell block. Petr was deported to Auschwitz, where he died in 1944.

Ilan was touched by the idea that a boy without freedom could still dream of flying to the moon. "I feel that my journey fulfills the dream of Petr Ginz fifty-eight years on," Ilan said. "A dream that is ultimate proof of the greatness of the soul of a boy imprisoned within the ghetto walls, the walls of which could not conquer his spirit. Ginz's drawings are a testimony to the triumph of the spirit."

Only later did Ilan learn that he had a personal connection to the picture. Petr's niece Tamar had been Ilan's classmate in high school.

Ilan also took a tiny Torah scroll with him into space. On a visit to the home of Professor Joachim Joseph, a scientist involved in the Mediterranean Israeli Dust Experiment to be performed aboard the spacecraft, Ilan asked about a tiny Torah he noticed on a bookshelf. Joseph told him that when he was a boy, he had been taken from his home in Holland and sent to the

Bergen-Belsen concentration camp. Rabbi Simon Dasberg, also from Holland, lived in the same barracks. Rabbi Dasberg learned that Joachim was approaching the age of Bar Mitzvah. He taught him to read his Torah portion from the tiny scroll the rabbi had smuggled into the camp. Following a secret Bar Mitzvah celebration in the barracks, Rabbi Dasberg, certain he would not survive the war, gave Joachim the Torah scroll for safekeeping. Joachim was freed and managed to save the Torah.

Ilan was inspired by the story. He told Professor Joseph that his own mother had been in a concentration camp during the war and had survived. Several months later, Ilan phoned the professor from Houston to ask if he could take the tiny Torah into space.

Ilan decided he would also carry an Israeli flag, an Israeli Air Force flag, a kiddush cup (a ceremonial wine cup), a T-shirt promoting Israeli road safety, Israel's Declaration of Independence, and a miniature Bible given to him by Israel's President Moshe Katzav.

Finally, Ilan chose a mezuzah, a small case holding parchment scrolls with Biblical verses, traditionally mounted on the doorpost of a Jewish home. He joked about attaching the mezuzah to the spaceship hatch.

Rona and the children gave him letters and photos,

**Professor Joachim Joseph's miniature Torah scroll
that Ilan took into space.**

and he took a necklace and watch to give them when he
returned.

Because he wanted to represent all Jews, Ilan decided
he would eat only kosher food on the flight, even
though he wasn't an observant Jew. NASA found a

food supplier who could package kosher food in bags suitable for preservation in space. "I am not going to eat pork or seafood despite the fact that the other astronauts have told me that shrimp cocktail is the most popular food in space," Ilan said.

★ Chapter 8 ★
DELAY

The astronauts were ready for takeoff. But over and over again, the launch, which was originally scheduled for 2001, was postponed because of technical problems or bad weather. The time in America stretched out. Though the Ramon family had come for two years, more than four had passed. Each time Ilan and the crew got ready, they learned that they'd have to wait. But Ilan stuck to his training. "I'm here to do a mission, and I'll stay until it's finished," he said.

In the meantime, the four Ramon children learned to speak English like Americans—with genuine Texas accents! They went to synagogue, to Hebrew school,

The Ramons, including *(from left, back row)* **Asaf, Rona, Ilan, Tal,** *(front row)* **Yiftah, and Noaa, take a family vacation in 1999.**

and to summer camp. One summer, Ilan and Rona joined their children at camp for a family vacation.

When Ilan was in the Israel Air Force, he would never talk to the press, because a pilot's work is considered secret. In Houston, Ilan cooperated with the many journalists who wanted to interview him and his family. He also spoke to local and national groups about his mission and became an ambassador of goodwill from Israel to the American community and the world.

"There is no better place to emphasize the unity of people in the world than flying into space," he said.

The Ramons liked their life in Houston, but they also missed Israel, and Ilan missed flying. When F-16's from a nearby air base flew over him, he looked up and wished he were sitting in the pilot's seat.

Ilan and Rona hoped the mission would take place soon. They wanted to be home in Israel for their son Tal's Bar Mitzvah.

★ Chapter 9 ★
BLAST OFF

At last, after many postponements, on January 16, 2003, Shuttle Mission STS-107 was ready to take off from Launch Pad 39-A in Cape Canaveral, Florida. The astronauts lay on their backs in bright orange pressure suits. Ilan was strapped in his seat in middeck. All systems looked good for launch. Outside the sun was shining and the sky was deep blue. Mission captain Rick Husband said, "The Lord has blessed us with a beautiful day."

The Jewish community was captivated by the idea of an Israeli astronaut and had come to know and love Ilan. In the crowd of spectators were many Jewish children.

One sixth-grade class chose to come to Cape Canaveral in place of their annual trip to Disney World. A boy from New Jersey received a trip to watch the launch for

The crew of the Columbia board the shuttle, January 16, 2003.
Ilan is in the second row, far left.

a Bar Mitzvah gift. Ilan's father and his brother Gadi came from Israel, though his mother was too sick to make the trip. In Israel the space flight was front page news and was broadcast live on radio and television.

At 10:38 A.M., the astronauts closed and locked their visors. Six seconds before takeoff, the main engines turned on. The shuttle rocked back and forth. The solid-fuel booster lit, and in a roar, Space Shuttle Columbia lifted off, leaving Planet Earth.

The Columbia Space Shuttle lifts off on January 16, 2003.

"It was very emotional," said his dad.

"I know he's laughing all the way up," Rona said of her husband, "because he is doing exactly what he wants to do."

Everything seemed to go smoothly, though the scientists on earth noticed one problem. While the Columbia was lifting off, a piece of insulation broke away from one of its fuel tanks and bounced off the left wing, which was covered with protective tiles. At this time, it was unclear if it had caused serious damage.

Eight and one-half minutes after liftoff, the engines shut down, and Space Shuttle Columbia began orbiting earth. "That's when Columbia ends being a missile and becomes a space laboratory," Ilan said.

Ilan's job was "payload specialist," which meant that he ran scientific experiments on board. Over 80 experiments were scheduled for the crew. Ilan's main experiment was to photograph and measure the movement of dust during desert storms to determine how it affects rain production and global warming. He also took six science experiments from students in Israel, Japan, China, and the United States.

One experiment, The Chemical Garden, was about how crystals grow in space. Students from ORT Middle School in Kiryat Motzkin near Haifa, Israel, selected

Ilan works with the STARS educational payload, whose experiments included "The Chemical Garden" developed by students in Israel.

cobalt and calcium so their crystals would be blue and white, the colors of their country's flag. On earth, crystals grow upward against gravity. How would they grow when free of gravity?

"What's exciting about this is that the students are the ones who had the idea, planned the experiment, participated in putting the hardware together, and of course, would analyze it postflight," Ilan said. "Space is a great tool to attract students to science."

Ilan, who had grown up in the desert, used a camera to study dust from the desert as the shuttle traveled over earth. He also captured "sprites," electronic charges on top of thunderheads. No one had ever studied that before.

In another experiment, he pedaled a bike while breathing in and out of a tube. Then he collected his breath to be analyzed after the mission ended.

For his first meal in space, Ilan ate kosher chicken and noodles, green beans with mushrooms, crackers, strawberries, trail mix, a brownie, and orange juice.

After the meal, the "Blue Team" of Willie McCool, Mike Anderson, and Dave Brown went to sleep, while the "Red Team" of Ilan, Rick Husband, Laurel Clark, and Kalpana Chawla stayed up.

Ilan started the science experiments. Finally, after a very long day, he and the other working astronauts woke their sleeping colleagues to take over so they could have a turn to sleep.

The space craft circled the earth at 17,500 miles an hour. The first time he flew over Israel and he could see Jerusalem, Ilan recited the Shema prayer, the Jewish affirmation that "God is One."

From space, he said, "Israel looks like it does on a map: small but charming. I think we have a great people in

Israel and we have to maintain our Jewish heritage."

On the spaceship, the sun rises and sets every 90 minutes, so Ilan asked a rabbi when he should celebrate the weekly Sabbath. They agreed he would follow Cape Canaveral time.

Crewmembers pose for a photo in the SPACEHAB Research Double Module. *(Clockwise from the bottom right):* **David M. Brown, Michael P. Anderson, Kalpana Chawla, and Ilan Ramon.**

Ilan liked being in space. "I wish I could stay longer, like you guys," Ilan told the three astronauts who were docked in the International Space Station.

He loved looking out the window, and he loved floating. "It is something like the magicians show us. It really is tremendous," he said. Watching their dad on TV, the Ramon children asked their father to do somersaults in the air.

But after a week in space, Ilan sent an e-mail to Rona. "Even though everything here is amazing, I can't wait until I can see you. A big hug for you and kisses for the kids."

One morning, the astronauts woke to a Hebrew song Rona sent Ilan. It was written by the Israeli poet Rachel:

Can you hear my voice, O my love afar?
Can you hear my voice, out there somewhere?
Crying out to you, crying deep in me,
Sending blessings down from a distant star.

On one of his breaks, Ilan took a call from Israel's prime minister, Ariel Sharon, which was broadcast live on television and radio.

All 16 wonderful days passed by quickly for Ilan. At 8:15 in the morning on Saturday, February 1, on its

Ilan and fellow astronauts take a call from Israel's Prime Minister Ariel Sharon *(center).*

255th orbit, Columbia slowed down to return to Earth. Ilan and the others took their seats and strapped themselves in. The space shuttle headed into the atmosphere.

Ilan's family waited for him below at Cape Canaveral, Florida, in a special viewing area.

But something went wrong. On entry into the earth's atmosphere, the outside of the space shuttle got too hot. Suddenly, on earth, instead of hearing the voices of the astronauts, there was silence from the Columbia.

Rona stood below and waited at the end of the runway for the landing. "It was a beautiful day," she said, "and the clock was ticking. When it got down to ten seconds, we started a countdown, just like at the liftoff. But the sonic booms didn't come. Then they took us aside and told us that they didn't know what had happened, but they had lost contact with the spacecraft. I didn't even have to tell the kids; they knew immediately that something was wrong."

In the sky above, the Space Shuttle Columbia burst apart, killing all seven crewmembers.

All over the world, stunned men, women, and children gasped in horror and broke down in tears. How could the seven wonderful astronauts be gone?

For Ilan's family and the families of the other astronauts, the loss was greater than for anyone else.

The Israeli government arranged a special flight to bring other family members from Israel to Florida, so they could be together at this terrible time. President George W. Bush offered the respect and gratitude of the people of the United States. "Some explorers," said the president, "do not return."

After memorial services in the United States, Ilan's body was flown back to Israel, where he was given a full

Israeli Prime Minister Ariel Sharon and Noaa, Rona, Yiftah, Tal, and Asaf Ramon sit together at Ilan's funeral.

military funeral. Many Israelis wept as they watched it on Israel TV. Asaf, 14, wore a blue flight jacket with a NASA patch and his father's name. Tal, 12, and Yiftah, 9, huddled close. Noaa, 5, sat on her mother's lap.

Struggling with her own grief, Rona gave them all courage. "Ilan went in search of a better world," she told them.

Prime Minister Ariel Sharon agreed. "On his last mission he soared higher than any other Israeli and realized his dreams," he said.

Ilan was laid to rest in a special place Rona chose: the

Jezreel Valley village of Nahalal, close to Ramat David Air Base, where he had served.

Rona said, "We and the families of the other astronauts are one big supporting family. We are bound in a magnificent way. The other crew members were close friends of Ilan's. The only thing that gives me any comfort is that they had such a good time and loved one another. They were simply a group of angels and that's how they will stay."

On the day of the burial, four F-16's saluted Ilan by flying above the small cemetery. As they approached, one veered upwards. A pilot was missing.

Around Ilan's grave grow red, pink, and purple cyclamens, a plant that renews itself year after year, pushing up over rocks in the winter when few flowers seek the sunshine. Above him are strong trees, mostly pine trees. The air smells wonderful. Higher, above the Nahalal farming silos, jet pilots practice against the blue sky.

★ Chapter 10 ★
REMEMBERING ILAN

In Hebrew and English, French and Russian, leaders of the world's nations as well as ordinary citizens signed memorial books at Israeli embassies and consulates around the world. Schoolchildren lit candles and said memorial prayers.

The Mediterranean Israeli Dust Experiment gathered unique data, according to Dr. Joachim Joseph, principal investigator, whose tiny Torah scroll had been lost in space. Even though the flight had been delayed to a time when dust storms are infrequent, Ilan succeeded in photographing clear images of dust plumes and sprites.

The students at the school in Kiryat Motzkin continue

to analyze photographs of the crystals they had sent up on the space shuttle. Their experiment had shown that on earth the cobalt and calcium fought gravity to grow upward, but in space the calcium crystals grew in the shape of a sphere, while the cobalt grew entwined like spaghetti.

The Chabad Jewish Community Center of the Space

General Jefferson D. Howell Jr., Johnson Space Center Director, and Rona Ramon, Ilan's wife, participate in a tree planting ceremony in memory of Columbia's crew members.

Coast in Florida is raising funds for a new Torah to replace the one Ilan brought into space. The sacred words of Jewish tradition will be read in his memory.

While in orbit, Ilan talked about the view of Planet Earth and the need to take care of it. "I think all of us have to keep it clean and good. It saves our life and gives us life," he said. Ilan called on every Jew in the world to plant a tree in the Land of Israel during the coming year. That would equal 13 million trees! In his memory, a grove of trees, or *ilanot* in Hebrew, was established by Jewish National Fund tree planters near Netanya. Other trees are being planted in parks, schools, and Air Force bases. The earth will be a more beautiful place because of Ilan Ramon.

And in space, each of seven asteroids bears the name of a Columbia crewmember. Above us, Asteroid Ilan Ramon is orbiting the sun between Mars and Jupiter.

Most of all, like the flowers that grow near his final resting place, Ilan showed that from the darkest moments of history, new growth and belief in the future can flourish. Even on dark days, the achievements of Israel's first astronaut, Ilan Ramon, assure us that when it comes to dreams, the sky is the limit.

The Columbia crew *(from left)*: David M. Brown, Rick D. Husband, Laurel B. Clark, Kalpana Chawla, Michael P. Anderson, William C. McCool, and Ilan Ramon

Timeline

June 20, 1954	Ilan Wolferman was born
1972	Graduated from Regional Himmelfarb High School, Beersheva
1973	Special Honor, Yom Kippur War
1974	Graduated Israel Air Force as combat fighter pilot
1976–80	Mirage III-C Flight Training
1980	F-16 Training Course, Hill Air Force Base, Utah
June 7, 1981	Operation Opera Mission to destroy Osirak nuclear reactor in Iraq
1982	Special Honor, Operation Peace for Galilee
1983-87	Tel Aviv University, B.A., Electronics and Computer Engineering
1986	Married Rona Bar Simantov
1992	Special Honor, F-16 10,000 Flight Hours
1994	Promoted to rank of Colonel, Israel Air Force

1995	U.S. President Clinton and Israel Prime Minister Peres announce joint space venture to include Israeli astronaut
1997	Ramon selected to participate in American space program
June 1998	Ramon family moves to Houston so Ilan can begin training
2001	Scheduled launch of mission
December 2002	Final dress rehearsal for mission
January 16, 2003	Space Shuttle Columbia launched
February 1, 2003	Columbia disintegrates in space. All seven members of crew perish.
February 12, 2003	Ilan Ramon buried at Moshav Nahalal, Israel

Index

Websites

<http://luna.tau.ac.il/~peter/MEIDEX/english.htm>
Description of Mediterranean Israeli Dust Experiment performed aboard Columbia spacecraft; memorial site to Ilan Ramon

<http://spaceflight.nasa.gov/shuttle/crew/intramon.html>
Preflight interview with Ilan Ramon

<http://www.israelnewsagency.com/israelastronautilanramon.html>
Photos, address by Prime Minister Ariel Sharon, opportunity to send condolences to Ramon family

<http://www.nasa.gov/columbia>
Crew profiles, mission overview, memorials

<http://www.science.co.il/Ilan-Ramon>
Biographical data, links to NASA

<http://www.us-israel.org/jsource/biography/Ilanramon.html>
Jewish Virtual Library—biography

This partially torn Israel Air Force flag belonging to Ilan was found in the debris from the Space Shuttle Columbia.

About the Author

Barbara Sofer is a prize-winning journalist and author, whose popular column is featured in The *Jerusalem Post* weekend edition. She is the Israel Director of Public Relations and Communications for Hadassah, the Women's Zionist Organization of America. As the liaison to the foreign press for Hadassah's Israel projects, she contributed to the Emmy-winning CNBC program *Jerusalem ER*. Her book *Kids Love Israel, Israel Loves Kids* has become the standard guidebook for families traveling in Israel. *Shalom, Haver, Goodbye, Friend,* a photo essay in memory of Israel's Prime Minister Yitzhak Rabin won the 1997 Sydney Taylor Award for the best Jewish childrens' book. Her adult novel *The Thirteenth Hour* won critical acclaim. The mother of five, Barbara lives in Jerusalem with her husband, scientist/writer Gerald Schroeder.

Photo Acknowledgments

Images in this book are used with the permission of: NASA, pp. 2–3, 31, 43, 44, 46, 48, 55, 57; © David Rubinger/CORBIS, p. 6; Milner Moshe/The State of Israel National Photo Collection, pp. 8, 20; Cohen Fritz/The State of Israel National Photo Collection, p. 10; The State of Israel National Photo Collection, p. 12; courtesy of Professor Reuven Segev, pp. 14, 16; used with permission of Rona Ramon, p. 15; Sa'ar Ya'acov/The State of Israel National Photo Collection, p. 22; © Getty Images, pp. 25, 28, 52, 64; AP/Wide World Photos, pp. 32, 62; Petr Ginz (1928–1944). *Moon Landscape*, 1943–1944. Pencil on paper. Gift of Otto Ginz. Collection of the Yad Vashem Art Museum, p. 34; © Joachim H. Joseph Ph.D., p. 37; © AFP/CORBIS, p. 40; Ohayon Avi/The State of Israel National Photo Collection, p. 50; courtesy of Karen Benzian, p. 63.

Front & back cover: courtesy of NASA.

Ilan salutes from the cockpit of his F-16 fighter jet.